Ramadan
and Eid al-Fitr

THIS EDITION

Produced for DK by WonderLab Group LLC
Jennifer Emmett, Erica Green, Kate Hale, *Founders*

Editor Maya Myers; **Photography Editor** Nicole DiMella; **Managing Editor** Rachel Houghton;
Designers Project Design Company; **Researcher** Michelle Harris; **Copy Editor** Lori Merritt;
Indexer Connie Binder; **Proofreader** Susan K. Hom; **Series Reading Specialist** Dr. Jennifer Albro;
Sensitivity Readers Imam Faizul Khan, Noor Ali, Ebonye Gussine Wilkins

First American Edition, 2025
Published in the United States by DK Publishing, a division of Penguin Random House LLC
1745 Broadway, 20th Floor, New York, NY 10019

Copyright © 2025 Dorling Kindersley Limited
25 26 27 28 29 10 9 8 7 6 5 4 3 2 1
001-349661-Sep/2025

All rights reserved.
Without limiting the rights under the copyright reserved above, no part of this publication may be reproduced, stored in or introduced into a retrieval system, or transmitted, in any form, or by any means (electronic, mechanical, photocopying, recording, or otherwise), without the prior written permission of the copyright owner.

DK values and supports copyright. Thank you for respecting intellectual property laws by not reproducing, scanning or distributing any part of this publication by any means without permission. By purchasing an authorised edition, you are supporting writers and artists and enabling DK to continue to publish books that inform and inspire readers. No part of this publication may be used or reproduced in any manner for the purpose of training artificial intelligence technologies or systems. In accordance with Article 4(3) of the DSM Directive 2019/790, DK expressly reserves this work from the text and data mining exception.

Published in Great Britain by Dorling Kindersley Limited

A catalog record for this book is available from the Library of Congress.
HC ISBN: 979-8-2171-2546-3
PB ISBN: 979-8-2171-2545-6

DK books are available at special discounts when purchased in bulk for sales promotions, premiums, fund-raising, or educational use.
For details, contact:
DK Publishing Special Markets, 1745 Broadway, 20th Floor, New York, NY 10019
SpecialSales@dk.com

Printed and bound in China
Super Readers Lexile® levels 500L to 610L
Lexile® is the registered trademark of MetaMetrics, Inc. Copyright © 2024 MetaMetrics, Inc. All rights reserved.

The publisher would like to thank the following for their kind permission to reproduce their images:
a=above; c=center; b=below; l=left; r=right; t=top; b/g=background
123RF.com: Nikjuzaili 11; **Adobe Stock:** Creatus 9bl, Gulfeye 20br, IndiaPix 14, Karrrtinki 18tr, Alisa Korolevskaya 26tl, Raul77 26br;
Alamy Stock Photo: ANP / Dominique Mollee 22, Johnny Armstead 24, Imaginechina Limited 27tr, Imago / Xinhua 27b, SOPA Images Limited 9tr, Xinhua 16b, ZUMA Press, Inc. 6, 21tr, ZUMA Press, Inc. / Amr Mostafa / APA Images 18br; **Dreamstime.com:** Antonel 15tr, Sener Dagasan 4-5, Ferli Achirulli Kamaruddin 23b, Nurlan Mammadzada 10, Mawardibahar 13, Satel22 20bl, Teacherphoto Photo 25clb, Tolgaildun 7tl; **Getty Images:** AFP / Fethi Belaid 16-17, AFP / Juni Kriswanto 28-29, AFP / Prakash Mathema 25cr, Anadolu 19, 23cra, Ulet Ifansasti 29cr, Moment / Maroot Sudchinda 7cr; **Getty Images / iStock:** E+ / Ibnjaafar 15b, E+ / SolStock 21b, E+ / Xavierarnau 3, Lakshmiprasad S 1; **Shutterstock.com:** Arapix 30, Sener Dagasan 12, Gergitek 8

Cover images: *Front:* **Adobe Stock:** Detshana t/ (Texture); **Dreamstime.com:** Buch (Background), Javid Hasanli cla; **Shutterstock.com:** Mrs_Ya; *Back:* **Dreamstime.com:** Javid Hasanli cl; **Shutterstock.com:** Kotoffei cra, clb

www.dk.com

This book was made with Forest Stewardship Council™ certified paper – one small step in DK's commitment to a sustainable future.
Learn more at www.dk.com/uk/information/sustainability

Level 2

Ramadan and Eid al-Fitr

Emma Carlson Berne

Contents

6	A Sacred Time
8	The Holy Month
10	The Prophet Muhammad
14	Marking Ramadan
18	Ramadan Around the World

20 Eid Celebrations
24 Eid Around the World
30 Glossary
31 Index
32 Quiz

Suleymaniye Mosque, Istanbul, Turkey

A Sacred Time

In Istanbul, Turkey, people gather to pray. The Hagia Sophia Grand Mosque is filled with people. Today is the first day of the holy month of Ramadan. It is a special time for Muslims around the world.

Worshippers stand together in the mosque. They bow their heads. Then, they bow to the ground to pray.

Understanding Islam

Islam is a religion that worships one god. This god is known as Allah. This is another name for the God worshipped in Judaism and Christianity. People who practice Islam are called Muslims. They believe the Prophet Muhammad was the last messenger of Allah. Islam began in what is now called the Middle East and North Africa. It has spread throughout the world. Islam is the world's fastest-growing religion.

The Holy Month

Ramadan is the ninth month of the Islamic calendar. This calendar is based on positions of the moon. Ramadan begins when the crescent moon appears. This is a month with many blessings.

During Ramadan, Muslims fast from dawn to sunset. They may go to the mosque to say special prayers. They also give money to charity. They work to strengthen their spirituality, kindness, and patience.

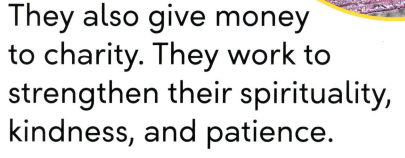

Fasting

Fasting is going without food or drink at certain times. Many Muslims fast as a sign of their devotion to God. Fasting can also be a way to remember people who are less fortunate.

The Prophet Muhammad

Long ago, the ninth month in the calendar was a holy time. Fighting was forbidden. People would meditate and think quietly. They often did this alone in the wilderness.

Muslims visiting the cave where the angel appeared

Who Was Muhammad?

Muhammad was the prophet of Islam. He was born in Mecca around 570 CE. (Mecca is now in Saudi Arabia.) During his lifetime, Muhammad and his followers spread the teachings of Islam. Muhammad died in 632 CE.

Muslims believe that the Prophet Muhammad meditated alone in a small cave. In 610 CE, Muhammad said an angel appeared. He said the angel spoke to him.

Muslims believe the angel spoke the words of God. These words became the first verses of the Qur'an. The Qur'an is Islam's holy book. The angel also revealed that Muhammad was a prophet. Prophets are believed to have been chosen to share God's message.

Inside the Cave of Hira

The night the angel spoke to Muhammad became known as the Night of Power. Muhammad began telling others that Allah had spoken to him. People believed Muhammad was a prophet. They began following him.

The name of the Prophet Muhammad in the Hagia Sophia

Ramadan was revealed to Muhammad as a month for fasting. Followers of Muhammad began fasting for the month in 624 CE.

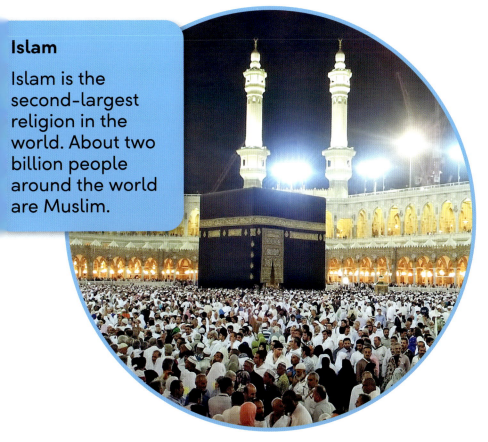

Islam

Islam is the second-largest religion in the world. About two billion people around the world are Muslim.

The most sacred site in Islam: the Kaaba at the center of the Masjid al-Haram, or the Great Mosque of Mecca, in Saudi Arabia

Marking Ramadan

During Ramadan, people fast between sunrise and sunset. They don't eat or drink during this time. Before the sun comes up, people eat an early meal. When the sun goes down, the household gathers for an evening meal. This meal is called iftar.

Exceptions to the Rule

Children are not required to fast during Ramadan. But some children choose to try it. Pregnant women, sick people, and people traveling are also excused from fasting.

Many Muslims eat dates to break their fasts. Muslims believe that the Prophet Muhammad ate dates when he was done fasting.

People may say extra prayers during Ramadan. Some spend more time studying the Qur'an.

People practice kindness. It is especially important not to gossip or say bad things about others. People try to do good deeds. They may work together to fill special boxes with food and supplies. They give these to people in need. Free meals are offered at community centers.

Volunteers pack meals in Cairo, Egypt

Ramadan Around the World

Muslims around the world observe Ramadan. In Egypt, children carry colored lanterns. Some people hang lanterns on the doors of their homes. A messenger bangs a drum in the streets before dawn. This wakes people up for the morning meal.

People bathing in the Cisadane River, Indonesia

People in part of Indonesia wash their hair in a river. They use a special shampoo made from rice straw. This makes them extra clean for the start of Ramadan.

Some people go to the mosque late at night for special prayers.

Eid Celebrations

The holiday of Eid al-Fitr marks the end of Ramadan. Families celebrate the end of fasting. They gather for special meals. They visit with friends. Adults may give children small gifts. People give money to the poor and the needy. They wish each other "Eid Mubarak," or "blessed Eid."

Sharing with Others

Muslims gather at the mosque on the morning of Eid al-Fitr. They pray Eid prayers together. They give money to a collection called Zakat al-Fitr. Zakat means "charity." This money is given to members of the community who need it. This helps everyone celebrate Eid al-Fitr.

Eid al-Fitr feasts help mark the end of Ramadan. In Arabic, Eid al-Fitr means "the festival of the breaking of the fast."

Bakeries make special sweets. Banners and decorations say, "Eid Mubarak."

People clean their houses. They wear new holiday outfits. Some visit the graves of relatives. They remember the dead.

Hello, Stranger!
Strangers greet each other on the street. They say, "Eid Mubarak!"

Eid Around the World

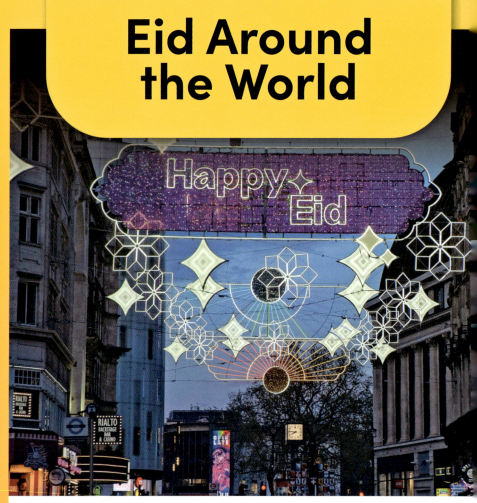

London, UK

Eid is a holiday for Muslims around the world. Families feast together. In some cities, people fill the streets. They enjoy parades and carnivals.

In some countries, people display brightly colored banners and flags. They hang colored lights.

Some women paint patterns on their hands with henna.

What a Cake!

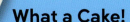

Families in Indonesia enjoy a special cake during Eid. This cake has between 15 and 30 layers! It is called lapis legit.

Eid al-Fitr brings feasts with friends and family.

Some people enjoy meat-stuffed dumplings called manti. They are popular in Armenia, Turkey, and Russia.

Sweet Treats

Sweets are a big part of Eid celebrations. In Turkey, the holiday is sometimes called the Sugar Feast!

Muslims in China may serve fried dough patties.

Cambaabur is a flat, tangy bread. It is a treat among Somali Muslims. At Eid, it's served with yogurt and sugar.

Eid al-Fitr snacks for sale in Yinchuan, China

The month of Ramadan is over. The night sky above Jakarta, Indonesia, is dark.

But the streets below are brightly lit. Thousands of happy people gather. It's time for an Eid al-Fitr parade.

In Indonesia, people bang drums. They wave flags. They chant and sing Eid songs. Children carry torches through the street. Loudspeakers boom messages of praise and joy.

It's time to celebrate! Eid Mubarak!

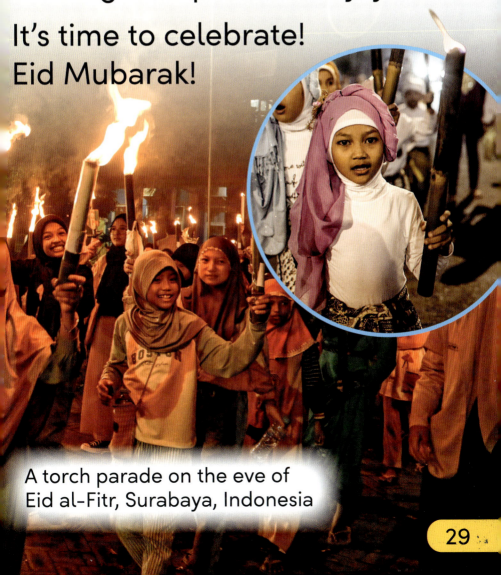

A torch parade on the eve of Eid al-Fitr, Surabaya, Indonesia

Glossary

Allah
God

Arabic
A language often spoken by people from Arab countries

Fast
To not eat or drink for a certain period of time

Henna
A reddish-brown dye that can be used to create temporary color on the hair or skin

Holy
Related to God or a god

Islam
A religion based on the teachings of Allah as told to the Prophet Muhammad

Islamic calendar
A lunar calendar Muslims use to decide the dates of holidays and other religious events

Mosque
A Muslim place of worship

Muslim
A person who practices Islam; relating to Islam

Qur'an
The holy book of Islam

Sacred
Holy

Spirituality
Concerned with religious values, something of a religious nature

Index

Allah 7, 12

charity (helping the needy) 9, 16, 20, 21

children 14, 18, 20, 29

China 27

Egypt 16, 18

Eid al-Fitr 20–29

fasting 9, 13–15, 20

feasts 22, 24, 26–27

henna 25

iftar 14

Indonesia 19, 25, 28–29

Islam 7, 13

Islamic calendar 8, 10

kindness 9, 16

mosque 6–7, 9, 13, 19, 21

Muhammad 7, 10–12

parades 24, 28–29

prayers 9, 16, 19, 21

prophets 11, 12

Qur'an 11, 16

Quiz

Answer the questions to see what you have learned. Check your answers in the key below.

1. During which month does Ramadan fall on the Islamic calendar?
2. What happened to Muhammad in 610 CE?
3. True or False: Fasting is a required part of Ramadan for small children.
4. What does "Eid al–Fitr" mean?
5. What is one way to greet someone during Eid al–Fitr?

1. Ninth 2. The Qur'an was revealed to him 3. False 4. "The festival of the breaking of the fast" 5. Hug them, say "Eid Mubarak"